VIDEO GAME
REVOLUTION

ESPORTS REVOLUTION

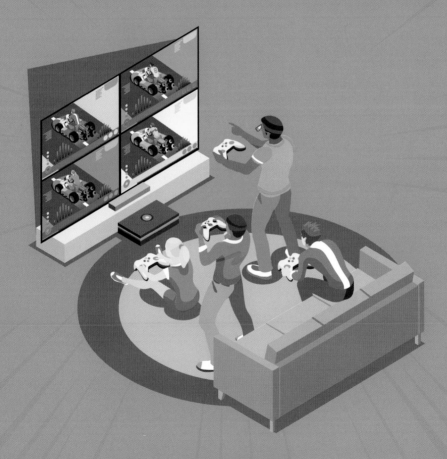

by Daniel Mauleón

CAPSTONE PRESS
a capstone imprint

Edge Books is published by Capstone Press,
1710 Roe Crest Drive, North Mankato, Minnesota, 56003
www.capstonepub.com

Library of Congress Cataloging-in-Publication Data
Names: Mauleón, Daniel, 1991- author.
Title: Esports revolution / by Daniel Mauleón.
Description: North Mankato, Minnesota : Capstone Press, 2020. |
Series: Edge books. Video game revolution | Audience: Age 8–14.
Identifiers: LCCN 2018059122 | ISBN 9781543571554 (hardcover) |
    ISBN 9781543571684 (ebook pdf)
Subjects: LCSH: Video games—Competitions—Juvenile literature.
Classification: LCC GV1469.3 .M3765 2020 | DDC 794.8—dc23
LC record available at https://lccn.loc.gov/2018059122

Editorial Credits
Gena Chester, editor; Kay Fraser and Rachel Tesch, designers; Tracy
Cummins, media researcher; Kathy McColley, production specialist

Photo Credits
Getty Images: Chung Sung-Jun, 5, Fairfax Media Archives, 7, KIM
JAE-HWAN/AFP, 13; Newscom: picture alliance/Frank May,
17; Shutterstock: Abdul Razak Latif, 29, Anna Chernova, Design
Element, aurielaki, Cover 1, Christos Georghiou, Design Element,
Designworkz, Design Element, Diana Grytsku, 15, Leonel Calara,
9, logoboom, 11, Mark Nazh, 21, Roman Kosolapov, 19, 22, 25, 27,
VectorPixelStar, Design Element, yurakr, Design Element

Printed and bound in the USA.
PA70

TABLE OF CONTENTS

WELCOME TO THE REVOLUTION

The Invictus Gaming, or iG, team members sat next to one another on a big stage in South Korea. Members had their own computers to play the video game. Across the stage in another booth was their **opponent** in the game, Fnatic. Both teams were surrounded by fans filling a 50,000-seat stadium.

Invictus Gaming celebrates winning the International *Dota 2* Championships.

The night started with an **augmented reality** music performance. More than 200 million people watched the performance—online and in person. There were fireworks, giant screens, and a dazzling trophy. Fans from around the world watched the teams compete for more than $800,000. Most were from China, rooting for iG, their country's team.

iG continued their game play, eventually defeating their opponent and winning the tournament. The camera cut inside the player booth. Song Eui-jin, who uses the **gamertag** "Rookie," was crying tears of joy. He was part of the first Chinese team to win the League of Legends World Championship. Even if you've never heard of it, the rise of esports is here.

augmented reality—an enhanced view of your surroundings that have been added to digitally

gamertag—a name players use online or in esports competitions

opponent—a person who competes against another person in a contest

THE EARLY DAYS OF ESPORTS

2

Since the beginning of video games, players have always tried to be the best. In **arcades,** players would compete for high scores in *Donkey Kong*, *Pac-Man*, and other games. The players with the highest scores left their initials on a **leaderboard.**

FACT!

Many arcade games were not programmed with endings. Instead the game would loop until an error prevented the players from beating the level. These are often referred to as kill screens.

Video games made their way into living rooms with the Magnavox Odyssey console. Soon friends and families competed. Some players wanted to be the best in the country.

During the 1970s Atari became a leader in video games. In 1980 it held the first National *Space Invaders* Tournament. More than 10,000 players entered in cities across the U.S. **Finalists** were given two hours to play the game *Space Invaders*. The winner with the highest score received an Atari tabletop video game.

Really Retro!

Magnavox released the first video-game console in 1972. The Magnavox Odyssey did not play sound and could only display black and white. To play, gamers twisted knobs on the controller. In 1977 the Atari 2600 was released. More than 25 million were sold. In 1985 the Japanese company Nintendo released its Nintendo Entertainment System (NES) in the U.S. The console launched with 17 games, including the best-selling *Super Mario Bros.* By 1990, 30 percent of houses in the U.S. owned the NES.

arcade—a place people go to play coin-operated games

finalist—someone who has reached the last part of competition

leaderboard—a list of highest scores with the names responsible for them for a specific game

SHOW ME YOUR MOVES! ★

As video games rose in popularity in the 1990s, competitive gaming did as well. Early competitions often centered around fighting games. Titles including *Street Fighter* and *Tekken* pitted two players against each other. Their characters would punch, kick, or shoot blasts of energy until they knocked out their opponent. To win, players memorized combos and practiced perfect timing.

The Evolution Championship Series (EVO) started in 1996. Originally it was called Battle by the Bay. Forty players gathered in an arcade in Sunnyvale, California. They competed in two different versions of *Street Fighter II*. At first, there were no prizes. But today, EVO players can compete for as much as $72,000. Now organizers select the most popular fighting games, from *Super Smash Bros.* to *Soulcalibur*, to play along with *Street Fighter II*.

FACT!

Street Fighter II has eight different versions since its original release in 1991. The original World Warrior version sold 6.3 million copies.

Street Fighter V is a game in the *Street Fighter* series.
It was released in 2016.

THE GAME CHANGER

3

The internet opened up many new avenues for the gaming community. It allowed players to share high scores, strategies, or events on forums. In the late 1990s, gamers used the internet to play each other online. In the 2010s players began **streaming** games to let other fans watch from around the globe.

BATTLING ONLINE

In May 1997 one of the earliest online tournaments began. It was called the Red Annihilation tournament. It tested the best players in *Quake*, a first-person shooter game played on the computer. During the first part of the tournament, about 2,000 players battled online. The top 16 players were invited to compete in person at the Electronic Entertainment Expo in Atlanta, Georgia. The winner took home a Ferrari, originally owned by a cocreator of *Quake*.

Today, the Electronic Entertainment Expo is held in Los Angeles, California.

THE BIRTHPLACE OF ESPORTS

In the 1990s South Korea became the first country to have nationwide internet. This type of internet was much faster than previous versions. Afterward internet cafés appeared around the country. These cafés were filled with rent-by-the-hour computers. People used them to play games online.

In 2000 the South Korean government started an esports division called the Korean e-Sports Association, or KeSPA. The division works to grow esports by managing it within the country. Soon South Korea had dedicated channels just for watching esports. KeSPA also created **leagues**, player and team resources, and more. Today many of the top players are South Korean. That's likely because of how long esports has been a part of South Korea's culture.

league—a group of esports teams that play against each other

FACT!
The strategy game *StarCraft* was one of the most popular games in South Korea when it was released in 1998. The best *StarCraft* players competed in the Ongamenet Starleague, one of the earliest esports leagues.

a *StarCraft* esports tournament

DREAMING UP A STREAM SCHEME

In 2007 Justin Kan and some friends built a website, plugged webcams into his computer, and launched Justin.tv. The website featured a 24/7 live stream of his house. It also had a chat room. People watching the stream could talk to each other or to Justin. Eventually, he opened up the site so others could have their own streams.

Video-game streams became popular on Justin.tv. But it was originally very expensive to get started. Streamers needed a lot of equipment. As time went on this equipment became cheaper. Soon more people began to stream video games.

By 2011 Justin.tv was renamed Twitch and became known for streaming games. Gamers would stream casual **playthroughs** of new games. During playthroughs some players provided tips, made jokes, or talked. Others would try to beat games as fast as possible. These gamers were called speed runners. Many talented streamers had a large number of viewers.

playthrough—the act of playing a video game from start to finish

Gamers often use headsets while they stream so they can talk to their viewers.

FRONT-ROW SEATS WHEREVER YOU SIT

As individual esports leagues and tournaments grew, many of them connected through Twitch. Today fans can use Twitch on the computer to watch the best gamers play at the same time as fans in the arena.

Many games and events are also streamed on YouTube. Countries such as China and South Korea have their own dedicated streaming sites. This works perfectly for fans who can't afford expensive tournament tickets. Now they can watch from the comfort of their living rooms.

FACT!
Every day more than 15 million people watch streams on Twitch. More than 2.2 million gamers stream each month on the site.

WORKING BEHIND THE SCREENS

4

Many different people make esports successful. Besides great players, esports events need great workers who make sure everything runs smoothly. There are many opportunities for fans who are interested in esports but don't have the skills to compete.

MEET THE PRODUCTION TEAM

Early on players ran many of the events. Today large tournaments and leagues have people who make sure cameras are rolling and lights are shining. Much like a TV studio or movie set, esports arenas have rooms just for the production team. In these rooms, TV screens cover an entire wall. Each screen shows a different camera view of the arena, screen, or player. The production team uses control panels. These panels are lit up with hundreds of buttons and switches. They allow the team to swap between cameras, change lights, or adjust volume.

Some events allow people to volunteer as backstage crew members. They help behind the scenes before, during, and after the event.

To fit its unique needs, esports offers some unique jobs. Instead of real cameras, virtual cameras live inside of video games. These cameras provide many different views of the game. They catch action up close. Only specially trained workers can control them. As an added bonus, since these esports cameras are virtual, they don't get in the way of the players.

The observer is the production team member who controls the virtual cameras. They tell the production team which cameras should be used so fans don't miss any of the action.

Better than the Movies

Companies are experimenting with new ways for viewers to enjoy esports. A company named Valve made a virtual reality, or VR, viewer for their game *Dota 2*. With a VR headset, fans can watch the game in two ways. A theater mode displays a larger-than-life screen in front of them. Another mode displays action as if the viewer was right in the game's battlefield. Either way, VR gives fans a unique viewing experience.

CASTING VOICES 🎙

Much like regular sports commentators, a caster provides information to an esports viewer. They talk throughout the action of the game. Whether you play the game or are watching your first match, casters help you understand what's happening.

Casters need to know as much as possible about a game, including details about characters and maps. They need to be able to explain player strengths and weaknesses, as well as their history in the game. Casters need to be entertaining. They may use jokes or wordplay to liven up their **broadcasts**.

Esports use two kinds of casters. Color casters use the breaks between action to explain why and how things are happening. Play-by-play casters take over when the game gets intense. Their goal is to help you understand who's doing what on-screen. Game play can be fast paced and hard to follow. Play-by-play casters explain the action as it happens so fans can keep up.

broadcast—to send out a program on TV, internet, or radio

MORE THAN ONE WAY TO WORK

There are a range of other jobs in the esports industry. Some are directly involved with gamers. Individual players or teams may have coaches who help them study or practice the game. If professional esports teams live together, they might even have a team chef. Analysts watch game play and provide advice to gamers. Some analysts even work for teams to learn about their opponents. Others work for leagues or tournaments and appear on broadcasts.

Just like with traditional sports, esports has journalists and photographers. Even big news companies such as ESPN have teams of esports reporters. Fans may run their own websites and podcasts to track games and players.

FACT!

Awards aren't just for players! Every year different companies award coaches, casters, game

ARE YOU A FAN?

Beyond players and esports staff, another important group is fans! They can enjoy all kinds of esports. Some fans will only watch the big matches each year. Others spend every day tracking stats about their favorite games.

cosplay—to creat[e] an event as a vid[eo] or TV character

The biggest fans are considered super fans. Super fans often watch streams of their favorite players. They attend live games and root for their favorite teams. They might even wear team gear or **cosplay** as characters from a game. Super fans love to share the joy of esports and are often welcoming to newcomers.

Fans cosplaying as Crystal Maiden, a character in *Dota 2*.

THE FUTURE OF ESPORTS

Compared to traditional sports, esports is still new. Each new event and each new league can change esports in a big way. It's slowly becoming more recognizable to those outside of the esports community. In 2018 esports was introduced as a demonstration sport at the Asian Games, a traditional sporting event. Esports will be a medal-winning contest at the 2019 Southeast Asian Games, the first time in the event's history.

In 2018, an international esports organization tried to get esports into future Olympic Games. But the president of the International Olympic Committee (IOC) noted that the violence in video games did not match Olympic values. Even so, esports does have some support in Olympic circles. And the IOC hasn't ruled out future involvement. As long as esports captures fans' interest, its future will be as exciting as the video games being played.

Malaysian fans cheering during
the Southeast Asian Games
opening ceremony

Glossary

arcade (ar-KAYD)—a place people go to play coin-operated games

augmented reality (awg-MENT-id ree-AL-uh-tee)—an enhanced view of your surroundings that have been added to digitally

broadcast (BRAHD-kast)—to send out a program on TV, internet, or radio

cosplay (KAHZ-play)—to create or dress up at an event as a video game, book, or TV character

finalist (FYE-nuh-list)—someone who has reached the last part of competition

gamertag (GAYM-ur-tag)—a name players use online or in esports competitions

leaderboard (LEED-ur-bord)—a list of highest scores with the names responsible for them for a specific game

league (LEEG)—a group of esports teams that play against each other

opponent (uh-POH-nuhnt)—a person who competes against another person in a contest

playthrough (PLAY-throo)—the act of playing a video game from start to finish

stream (STREEM)—to share footage online of video-game play; some streams are done live

Read More

eSports: The Ultimate Gamer's Guide. New York: HarperCollins Publishers, 2018.

Marquardt, Meg. *Great E-Sports Debates.* The Great Sports Debates. Minneapolis: Abdo Pub., 2018.

Polydoros, Lori. *Awesome Video Game Competitions.* Cool Competitions. North Mankato, MN: Capstone Press, 2018.

Internet Sites

ESPN
www.espn.com/esports/

Super League
www.superleague.com/

The Video Game Revolution
www.pbs.org/kcts/videogamerevolution/

Index